D0574549

CRIME SCENE SCIENCE

In the Laboratory

By Barbara J. Davis

Science and curriculum consultant:
Suzy Gazlay, M.A., science curriculum resource teacher
Consulting forensic scientist:
Carmen McIntire, Forensic Scientist,
The Mississippi Crime Lab

WORLD ALMANAC® LIBRARY

The publisher extends a big thank you to Carmen McIntire, forensic scientist; The Mississippi Crime Lab; and science educator Suzy Gazlay.

Please visit our web site at: www.garethstevens.com
For a free color catalog describing World Almanac® Library's list of high-quality books and multimedia programs, call 1-800-848-2928 (USA) or 1-800-387-3178 (Canada). Gareth Stevens Publishing's fax: (414) 332-3567

Library of Congress Cataloging-in-Publication Data available upon request from publisher. Fax (414) 336-0157 for the attention of the Publishing Records Department.

ISBN-13: 978-0-8368-7711-3 (lib. bdg.)
ISBN-13: 978-0-8368-7716-8 (softcover)

3764 9521 6/08

This North American edition first published in 2007 by
World Almanac© Library
A Member of the WRC Media Family of Companies
330 West Olive Street, Suite 100
Milwaukee, WI 53212 USA

ticktock project editor: Ruth Owen
ticktock project designer: Jane Massey
ticktock picture researcher: Lizzie Knowles
World Almanac© Library editorial direction: Mark J. Sachner
World Almanac© Library editor: Tea Benduhn
World Almanac© Library art direction: Tammy West
World Almanac© Library graphic designer: Dave Kowalski
World Almanac© Library production: Jessica Yanke and Robert Kraus

Picture credits
t = top, b = bottom, c = center, l = left, r = right, OFC = outside front cover, OBC = outside back cover
Alamy: 17t. BrandXpictures: 39b. Corbis: 19c. Andrew Davidhazy School of Photographic Arts and Sciences/RIT: 20l. Nichol Jennings: 9t. Mikael Karlsson/arrestingimages.com: 7t, 12t, 14b, 19t, 23t, 23b, 24. Keygrove Marketing Ltd www.keygrovemarketing.co.uk: 6t, 9br, 19tr, 41l, 45tr. Rex Features: 13bl, 13br. Science Photo Library: 5br, 6b, 8, 10b, 13t, 16b, 18, 22, 27b, 28, 31, 32, 33, 34, 35t, 38, 46. Shutterstock: 1, 3, 4all, 5t, 5c, 5bl, 7b, 9bl, 11all, 12c, 12b, 14t, 16t, 17b, 19b, 20br, 21r, 25, 26b, 27t, 29b, 30all, 35b, 36all, 37all, 40all, 41r, 42t, 43all, 44all, 45bl, 45br, 47all. ticktock Media Picture Archive: 26t, 29t, 39t. Wikipedia: 21l.

Printed in Canada

1 2 3 4 5 6 7 8 9 10 10 09 08 07 06

Contents

Crime labs analyze many types of crime scene evidence. In the case of a fire, the evidence might include burned pieces of cloth, charred wood, even samples of melted plastic.

It looks like a tough case. A man lies dead in a burned-out building. The crime scene investigators have only been able to recover a piece of charred fabric from his corpse. The detectives wish they had more, but they are confident that the next step in the investigation will turn up some much needed answers—the evidence sample is on its way for analysis at the crime lab.

Analyzing the evidence

The crime lab (short for *laboratory*) is a place where forensic scientists known as criminalists analyze a piece of evidence and deduce more information from the sample than you might think is possible. The professionals working in a crime lab have a very important responsibility. Interpreting physical evidence correctly can make the difference between bringing a criminal to justice and that criminal going free. The opposite is equally true. Correctly interpreting evidence can help prevent an innocent person from being wrongfully convicted.

Crime labs use scientific methods to analyze and interpret the evidence that is brought in. A wide variety of sciences are used every day in the crime lab. In fact, biology, chemistry, physics, and computer science might all be used to analyze just one piece of evidence.

A crime lab may be staffed by a number of different scientists, each specializing in analyzing one type of evidence, or by just one person who is trained

Microscopes and other specialized laboratory equipment allow forensic scientists to take a very close look at crime scene evidence. The evidence from a fire may be used to tell when a fire started and whether or not it was an accident.

If a crime lab sample is part of a human skeleton, forensic anthropology (the study of human bones) will be used to analyze the sample.

to run a number of different types of tests. Whether a small, one-person lab or a huge enterprise staffed by hundreds, a crime lab is an exciting place to be.

In this book, you will have the chance to step inside the crime laboratory and enter the world of the forensic scientist. You will explore the methods used to analyze the many different objects that are considered crime evidence: from bullets to fingerprints, blood stains to dog hairs! And, you will also have a chance to read about true-life cases where the scientific skills of criminalists helped to solve crimes and put perpetrators behind bars. Ready to see how it's done?

Welcome to the crime laboratory!

A simple cigarette butt is likely to have traces of the saliva of the person who smoked the cigarette. The DNA in the saliva can be identified using advanced laboratory analysis techniques. DNA evidence is very valuable because it can prove that a particular person was present at a crime scene.

AT THE CRIME SCENE

Crime Scene Investigators (C.S.I.s) seal off a crime scene then begin the slow and careful search for evidence.

- The crime scene photographer documents the scene and all the evidence before it is collected.

- Evidence is collected and then bagged and tagged (labeled) for the lab.

- Tiny items, such as single hairs and fibers, are collected using tools such as tweezers.

- Samples of blood are collected using swabs on sticks (like the swabs used at a doctor's office).

- A piece of clothing, a soda can, even a cigarette butt could turn out to be a key piece of evidence—they all are collected and taken to the crime lab.

Evidence is often transported using metal containers that do not absorb any liquid present in the sample. Metal containers also provide protection for fragile evidence like burned, flaky material from a fire.

Inside the crime laboratory, it is quiet and cool. You see a person dressed like a surgeon standing at a table, sorting through human skeleton bones. From behind a closed door, you hear the muffled sound of gunshots. All around you, scientists are using laboratory equipment to analyze evidence collected from crime scenes.

The scientific process

All crime labs share one important characteristic: They are places where the scientific method is used in the investigation of crimes. The evidence that the crime lab is investigating may be a strand of hair or a paint chip from a vehicle. Whatever it is, the sample will go through a basic scientific process: observation, hypothesis, experimentation, data collection, and the drawing of a conclusion.

Today, a metal container holding the burned piece of cloth from the fire arrives in the crime lab. The crime scene investigation report shows that a person was killed in the fire and that detectives think it was set on purpose. Intentionally setting a fire is a crime called arson. Because a person was killed in the fire, it is also a homicide. Both of these crimes are very serious offenses. The crime lab will try to determine whether the piece of burned cloth (the evidence sample) points to arson or an accidental fire.

Observation & hypothesis

At the crime scene, the C.S.I. team carries out the first two steps in the scientific process of observation and hypothesis. Their crime scene report shows that the evidence sample was

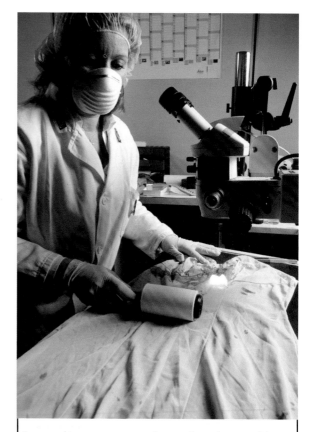

Even something as common as an adhesive roller can be very useful in a crime laboratory. It can be used to collect hair and clothing fibers from a blood-stained dress. Further analysis may link the evidence to a suspect, placing that person at the crime scene. Protective clothing and gloves are worn by crime lab technicians to prevent contamination of the evidence.

A knife with blood on it provides several sources of possible evidence. Prints can be lifted from the knife and analyzed to identify the person who held it. Testing the blood on the blade will determine if the knife was used to stab a particular victim.

〰〰〰〰〰〰〰〰〰〰〰

SCIENCE STEPS

Like all good scientists, crime lab technicians follow the scientific method.

- **Observation:**
  Carefully examine the evidence and the crime scene report. Identify the evidence.

- **Hypothesis:**
  Based on the crime scene report and the evidence observation, make a hypothesis about what the evidence is and what it may represent.

- **Experimentation:**
  Perform the tests needed to prove the hypothesis.

- **Data collection:**
  Record everything that happens during the experiment and the test results.

- **Drawing a conclusion:**
  Examine the test results to see if the hypothesis is correct.

observed and found in the lowest part of the burned-out area. This area usually indicates where the fire started. In fact, the report states that there seem to have been several places where the fire might have started. Because most fires don't start in several places at once, the finding points toward the possibility of arson. The hypothesis is now arson.

Fires that are started need some type of material called an accelerant—a chemical, gas, or other flammable material that will catch fire if it comes into contact with a flame or other source of very high temperature. Even though the sample is burned, traces of the accelerant might be found if you know how to look. The crime lab technicians certainly do! They take over the next step in the scientific process: experimentation.

Experimentation

Crime labs use technologically advanced equipment to analyze certain materials. First, the crime lab decides what types of tests will be run on the piece of burned cloth. The lab may test to see if some type of flammable oil or chemical is on the cloth. They may also run tests to identify the exact materials the cloth is made of. Each type of test requires that an evidence sample be prepared in a particular way. Each type of test may also have several steps. Once a sample is prepared, the tests will be run, and the results of each step in those tests will be carefully recorded to ensure that the data collection is accurate.

Fabrics burn at different rates. Tightly woven wool burns slowly. Cotton burns quickly. Synthetic materials, such as polyester, actually melt! These particular qualities can help crime lab technicians identify a fabric found at a crime scene.

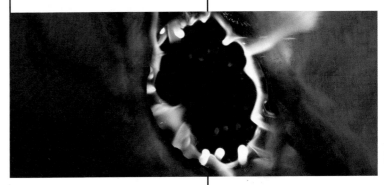

Forensic scientists know that any evidence that is not handled properly will be useless in a court of law.

Later in this book, we will take a closer look at the ways in which different types of evidence are prepared for specific tests.

Data collection & conclusion

With the tests completed and any data collected, the crime lab technicians can now interpret the data and draw a conclusion about the chemicals and other materials that are in the evidence sample.

As it turns out, in this particular case, the crime scene investigators were exactly right. Analyzing the piece of burned cloth has picked up traces of gasoline. Someone definitely started the fire.

Tracking evidence

Crime scene evidence is so important to successfully bringing an offender to justice that no chances can be taken on the possibility of evidence getting lost after it arrives at the crime lab. Also, there can be no possibility that anyone during the trial of a suspect can accuse the crime lab of mishandling the evidence. Crime labs rely on a detailed evidence log, which is a record-keeping system that tracks each person that handles the evidence and every test performed on the evidence.

Contamination

Accuracy, accuracy, accuracy! Whatever the crime lab learns through its experiments had better be correct. A great deal depends on the truth of the information uncovered during the lab tests. One thing that can really hurt the value of evidence tests is if the evidence is somehow contaminated with materials that

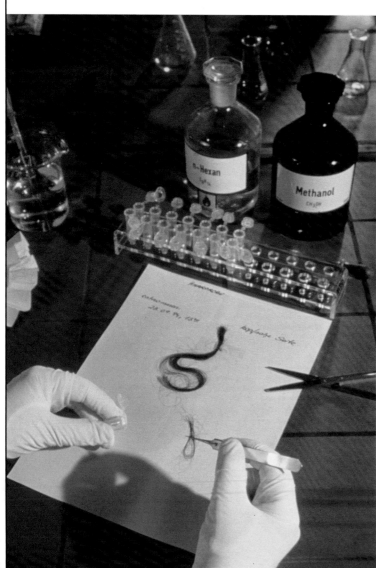

Evidence samples are prepared for testing in different ways. Here, a hair sample from a suspected drug abuser is being prepared for analysis. As hair grows, it takes in traces of chemicals produced when drugs in the body are broken down. These chemicals stay in a fixed position in the hair shaft, so a lock of hair cut from near the scalp can be used to reveal the history of a drug user's habits over a period of weeks. This hair sample is being cut into 0.5-inch pieces that correspond to specific dates.

A technician has used tweezers to remove a bullet from an evidence bag. Everything the technician observes about the bullet will be recorded. This information might include identifying marks or the presence of fingerprints. When the technician finishes, she will place the bullet back into the evidence bag.

don't belong there. In the arson case, for example, a dog hair from the leg of the crime scene investigator's pants doesn't belong in the metal container with the piece of burned cloth. If the dog hair isn't noticed by someone in the lab, it might throw off the results of chemical tests on the cloth. In the lab itself, being careless in removing the sample from its container may also cause contamination. Even the smallest trace of a simple lab chemical could throw off the accuracy of the test results.

Each person who takes possession of these bullets from a crime scene must record that he or she has done so on a "chain of possession" document. The document will identify everyone, from a person carrying the evidence from one lab to another, to the technicians performing the tests.

CHAIN OF POSSESSION

Received from:		
By:		
Date:	Time:	AM/PM
Received from:		
By:		
Date:	Time:	AM/PM
Received from:		
By:		
Date:	Time:	AM/PM
Received from:		
By:		
Date:	Time:	AM/PM
Received from:		
By:		
Date:	Time:	AM/PM
Received from:		
By:		
Date:	Time:	AM/PM

THE EVIDENCE LOG

The evidence sample arrives at the crime lab. The crime lab technician records:

- Evidence number (this can be assigned by the C.S.I. or the crime lab).
- Description of the evidence.
- Date and time.
- Name of person taking the evidence into the lab.
- Type of tests requested.

The evidence sample is placed in temporary storage until it can be tested. Sometimes, this is a refrigerator. Normally, two people record the following:

- Description/date/time.
- The fact that the sample was placed in the refrigerator.

When the evidence sample is removed from storage for testing, the crime lab technician records:

- Name of the person removing it.
- Date and time.

When the evidence sample is delivered for testing, the technician records:

- Date and time.
- The test results.
- Date and time the tests ended.
- Date and time the evidence sample is returned to storage.

A crime lab technician can compare boot prints found at a crime scene with images stored on manufacturers' databases of sole patterns.

A tour of the crime lab

Crime labs may be run by private businesses, government agencies, or even universities that sometimes offer their services to local law enforcement agencies.

The world's largest crime lab is operated by the U.S. Federal Bureau of Investigation (FBI). Its crime lab includes units that specialize in particular types of science or analysis. An arson sample might go to a Physical Sciences unit to be tested for the presence of gasoline or other accelerant. Blood and hair samples might go to a Biology or Trace Evidence unit to be tested for the presence of drugs, poisons, or carbon monoxide gas. A bullet pried from the wall at a crime scene would probably go to a Firearms and Ballistics unit. A possible poisoning case? The evidence sample would go to Toxicology.

The Impression Evidence unit might analyze a boot print or a tire track, or even a window frame that looks like it might have been gouged in the process of a burglar breaking into a house. A skilled crime lab technician can identify the type and size of tool that created the gouge. That information could provide the link to finding the person responsible for the crime.

An evidence sample may actually travel through more than one of these specialized labs. A bloodstained piece of clothing might go first to the DNA-testing area where some of the blood would be removed for testing. The sample might then travel on to the Trace Evidence unit to have the cloth fibers analyzed.

The FBI crime lab also has units that use advanced photography techniques like 3-D imaging to help solve crimes. A 3-D photographic method allows images to have depth. This technique can

The FBI's Serology Lab is responsible for analyzing blood samples. The scientist to the left is examining a handgun for traces of blood. The scientist to the right is dissolving a blood clot to prepare it to be analyzed for blood group or for DNA information.

IN THE LAB—DOs AND DON'Ts

DOs—Crime lab technicians should:

- Wear disposable gloves at all times when handling evidence bags and never touch evidence with their bare hands.

- Use tweezers, forceps, or other instruments to handle evidence samples instead of handling evidence with their fingers.

- Wear lab coats over regular street clothes.

- Wear protective eyewear when handling evidence, such as blood or chemicals.

DON'Ts—Crime lab technicians should not:

- Bring food or drinks into areas where evidence is being handled or tested.

- Touch gloved hands to their face or hair when working with evidence.

- Forget to log the date and time the evidence is in their possession.

- Leave evidence unattended.

be used to reconstruct an entire evidence sample from a partial one. For example, parts of an exploded bomb might be analyzed to see what the whole bomb looked like before it went off.

Questioned documents

A crime lab may have a unit that specializes in analyzing forged documents and handwriting. "Questioned documents" is the FBI's term for any kind of document that might be forged. Like a person's fingerprint, the way in which a person writes can identify that person. Unlike a fingerprint, though, handwriting can sometimes be copied so well that fake documents are created. Why would anyone want to copy

another person's handwriting? Imagine finding a letter signed by Abraham Lincoln. A historical document like that would be worth a great deal of money. Sometimes people try to create such a letter and pass it off as the real thing. Other forgeries would be of a not-so-famous person's signature—such as a person signing a check for a very large amount! When a person writes a word or words, they angle and space the letters in a particular way. They also shape them in a unique fashion. A handwriting analyst will use a magnifying glass or a microscope to look at these characteristics. They will even measure the actual distance between letters and the angle of each letter.

This hot dog and cup of soda are packed with chemicals—they are a major potential source for evidence contamination. Food and drinks can ruin evidence by adding substances that don't belong with the evidence.

It isn't as easy as you might think to perfectly copy a signature. Crime lab handwriting analysts examine all the details of how each and every letter was formed. They even analyze how hard the writer pressed down on the paper to form the words.

Tools of the trade

In 1910, Dr. Edmond Locard opened the doors of the world's first crime laboratory in Lyon, France. Dr. Locard was the director of the technical police laboratory there. He believed that every crime scene had evidence of the perpetrator if only it could be found and analyzed. If you were to visit Dr. Locard's laboratory, it wouldn't look much like a modern science lab, but there would be one device that you would be likely to recognize right away—the microscope. Today, microscopes are still one of the most important tools for studying many different types of evidence—although they are far more powerful than the ones used in the first crime lab!

Microscopes are able to make even the tiniest sample large enough to examine, and they are able to produce images that allow a jury to see small details on a piece of evidence.

In larger crime labs, gas chromatographs and mass spectrometers are two of the most commonly used instruments. A chromatograph separates a sample into its individual chemical components, or parts. A spectrometer identifies each chemical component and calculates exactly how much of that component is present in the sample. Both instruments use line graphs to show the data. One or both of these instruments are used to analyze the composition of a very wide variety of materials. These materials include: fire accelerants, blood, paint, ink, even fabrics. The instruments are also very accurate. For example, if the correct type of chromatograph is used to analyze a sample that contains gasoline, the graph may show whether the gasoline is regular or premium!

Microscopes, chromatographs, and spectrometers are just three of an amazing selection of high-tech pieces of equipment used in today's crime labs. However, even everyday objects like tweezers, rulers, tracing paper, cotton swabs, and fingernail polish remover are important crime lab tools playing their part in the investigation of evidence.

Bloodstained clothing can be examined by several different crime lab units. This shirt shows evidence of stabbing so, along with the bloodstain analysis and possible fiber analysis, the tear in the shirt will be examined to try to identify the type of weapon used.

Hand-held magnifying lenses have been an important scientific tool for hundreds of years. Today's crime labs may have hand-held lenses in a variety of sizes and powers of magnification.

Whatever the evidence, a microscope is likely to be a critical part of the evidence examination process. Some microscopes, like the one to the left, have one eyepiece. The magnification can be changed by moving the lenses above the sample plate.

A colored scanning electron micrograph shows diatoms present on the clothing fibers of a suspected burglar. Diatoms are microscopic single-celled algae. They are important to crime lab analysis because different species live in particular areas. The types of diatoms found on a piece of evidence can suggest where the evidence has been. Diatoms can help link suspects, victims, and crime scenes.

A CAREER IN CRIME SCIENCE
PROFILE: THE FBI FORENSIC SCIENCE RESEARCH AND TRAINING CENTER

Along with the world's largest crime lab, the FBI also runs the Forensic Science Research and Training Center. Here, FBI agents and FBI lab technicians are taught how to use the most advanced scientific technologies and methods to help them correctly analyze evidence.

New agents or laboratory professionals take classes such as biochemistry, physics, genetics, and chemistry. Other students might be experienced technicians and scientists who come to the center to take more advanced courses in specialist subjects such as arson, bombing, DNA analysis, document analysis, firearms identification, footwear identification, microscopy, and photography.

Crime labs are relying more and more on high-technology instruments to analyze evidence. Because of this equipment, the Forensic Science Research and Training Center also offers classes on how to best use the latest instruments.

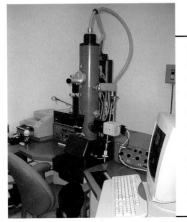

Scanning electron microscopes (SEMs) can show the surface of an object, the shape and size of particles that make up the object, even the basic elements of which the object is made. Some scanning electron microscopes can magnify an image to 200,000 times its original size! The 3-D image is viewed on a computer screen.

09-11-01

THIS IS NEXT
TAKE PENACILIN NOW

DEATH TO AMERICA
DEATH TO ISRAEL

ALLAH IS GREAT

Crime lab technicians learn how to analyze evidence documents such as this letter contaminated with anthrax (a bacterial disease). It was sent to NBC TV in New York City.

In 1910, Thomas Jennings broke into a home and shot the homeowner. Jennings didn't pay attention to the fact that he had put his hand on wet paint. However, the police investigating the crime paid quite a bit of attention to those prints. In fact, they used them as evidence during Jennings's trial.

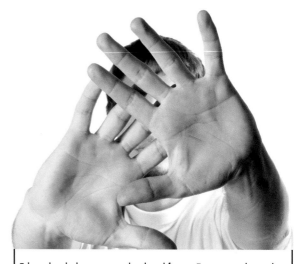

Take a close look at your own hands and fingers. Try counting the number of ridges and spaces in your fingertips and palms. A skilled fingerprint analyst looks at hundreds of points of reference when comparing unknown fingerprints with a known example.

This was the first time that "fingerprint analysis" was used in the United States to help convict a criminal. It became the leading tool for identification as soon as scientists discovered that each person's fingerprints are "one of a kind."

Arches, whorls, and loops

The skin on the undersides of a person's hands and feet is covered with tiny ridges and valleys. The ridges may divide, cross, or simply end. All this dividing and crossing forms complex patterns. As hard as it may be to believe, each fingertip on a person's hands has a different pattern. Those patterns are also different from any other person's fingertip pattern. If you think about the billions of people in the world, you might get an idea of just how many different fingerprints exist!

How can crime lab technicians hope to match a partial fingerprint lifted from a crime scene? They rely on skilled observation, and they use a system to do a step-by-step analysis of the print.

Arches, whorls, and loops might sound like features on an amusement park roller-coaster. However, they are actually words that are used to describe fingertip ridge patterns. Fingerprints are divided into eight general pattern categories, which are based on whether some or all of the ridge patterns are present. Some of the categories combine patterns, such as the "double-loop" whorl.

In addition to arches, whorls, and loops there are other characteristics in fingerprints called

Sometimes, fingerprint evidence arrives in the crime lab on a weapon, such as this knife. It might even arrive on an entire window removed from a crime scene or the rear view mirror taken out of a car!

TIMELINE: A HISTORY OF FINGERPRINTING

- In the 1830s, a Prussian professor named Johannes Purkinje defined a fingerprint classification system. He identified nine basic types of fingerprints.

- By the 1880s, Sir Henry Faulds, a Scottish doctor, and other researchers believed that each person's fingerprints were unique. This meant fingerprints could be used to identify an individual.

- In 1892, Sir Francis Galton, a British scientist, published a book about fingerprints which included the fact that they are unique and remain the same throughout our lives.

- In the late 1800s, Sir Edward Henry, the head of the Metropolitan Police agency in London, England, came up with a fingerprint classification system that allowed fingerprints to be logically filed according to their ridge characteristics. The stystem we use today is based on Henry's work.

FINGERPRINT CLASSIFICATIONS

There are eight main fingerprint pattern types.

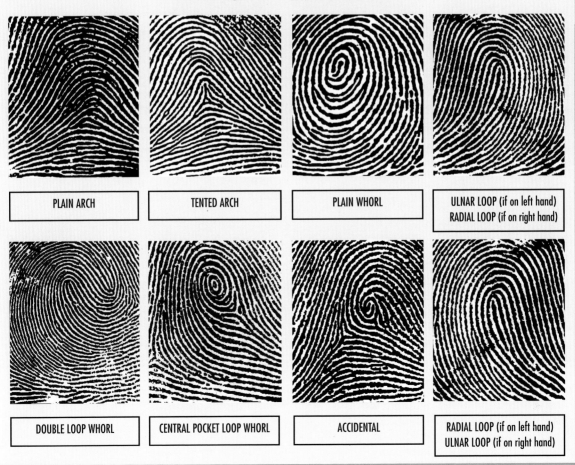

PLAIN ARCH	TENTED ARCH	PLAIN WHORL	ULNAR LOOP (if on left hand) RADIAL LOOP (if on right hand)
DOUBLE LOOP WHORL	CENTRAL POCKET LOOP WHORL	ACCIDENTAL	RADIAL LOOP (if on left hand) ULNAR LOOP (if on right hand)

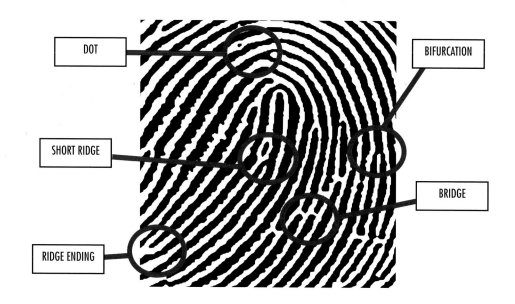

DOT

BIFURCATION

SHORT RIDGE

BRIDGE

RIDGE ENDING

minutiae. These characteristics include lakes, ridge endings, bifurcations, dots, and bridges.

Analyzing the prints

Fingerprints are collected at the crime scene by the C.S.I. team. Prints are brushed with a colored powder to make them visible. Then they are photographed or "lifted" (using sticky tape) and stuck to a card. The photograph, card, or piece of evidence arrives at the crime lab, and that is what the examiner will work from.

At the crime lab, the first step is to analyze and classify the print according to all the pattern variations.
Quite a task!

Is the print whorled or not? If so, what type of whorl is it and how many whorls are there?

Analyzing a fingerprint lifted from a crime scene doesn't do much good, though, unless it can be used to identify the person who left it behind.

Evidence prints are considered "unknown prints." The examiner knows the prints belong to someone—they just don't know who! To try and solve that mystery, unknown prints are compared to "known prints."

Perhaps this burglar thought fingerprints couldn't be lifted off a piece of fruit! An invention called magnetic fingerprint powder is making it easier to find and analyze prints left on difficult surfaces such as plastic bags, magazine covers, wallpaper... and banana peels. Tiny iron flakes with an organic coating stick to the greasy residue in a fingerprint. Excess powder is removed by a magnet instead of the usual brushing.

Crime lab fingerprint examiners rely on high quality print impressions to help them correctly analyze print evidence. Law enforcement officers are trained in the correct way to "roll" a finger in the ink to get as complete a print as possible.

Comparing prints

Known prints have been identified as belonging to a particular person. Hundreds of thousands of prints have been scanned into one of several national fingerprint databases. These fingerprints have been collected under a number of circumstances: People entering the United States are fingerprinted; U.S. citizens planning on traveling to other countries are fingerprinted; prints are taken from those who have been arrested. To compare an unknown print to these thousands of known prints, crime labs rely on a very important information source—an Automated Fingerprint Identification System (A.F.I.S.) which runs on a computer database.

A CAREER IN CRIME SCIENCE
PROFILE: FINGERPRINT EXAMINER

Latent print examiners often work at crime scenes looking for prints that might not be visible to the unaided eye. They use the latest "lift" technology, including regular, fluorescent, and magnetic powders, lifting tape, cards, brushes, and a camera. However, getting the prints is only part of a print examiner's very important job.

Back at the crime lab, the print examiner will first log in the arrival of the print evidence and then will make sure it is safely stored until he or she can further examine it. Then, the examiner will take a very close look at the evidence prints. Later, the prints will be compared to fingerprint examples called up from the AFIS database and other sources.

Latent fingerprint examiners may also prepare court exhibits that feature the evidence fingerprints. They also act as expert witnesses during court trials.

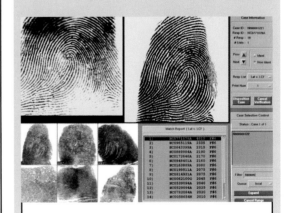

Automated Fingerprint Identification Systems (A.F.I.S.) are a method of storing, searching, and retrieving fingerprints held in a computer database. Within minutes, an A.F.I.S. will offer a fingerprint examiner a number of likely matches found within the database.

A crime lab fingerprint examiner will use a hand-held scanner to scan the image of the unknown print and enter it into the database. Within minutes, the computer searches all its records for possible matches. In a single fingertip, as many as 300 points of comparison need to be compared. The A.F.I.S. produces a series of a few prints that are close matches to the unknown print. The matches are then displayed on a high-resolution monitor, ready for the final step. This is the examination by an expert crime lab fingerprint analyst.

The analyst will very closely and carefully examine the images on the screen. The skill of the analyst is critical at this point. If even one point of comparison is dissimilar, the evidence print may no longer be useful. When the analyst is satisfied that the unknown print either does or does not match known prints, he or she will prepare a detailed report for the police.

Perfect match

"It's a 90% match!" the TV detective says about the lab results from a crime scene fingerprint. Exciting as that idea may be, it's also totally wrong. There is no such thing as a fingerprint that nearly matches another print. For a fingerprint to be of any use as evidence, it must be a complete match with a known fingerprint. The known fingerprint may come from a database or from the finger of a suspect. However the known fingerprint is obtained, there is no margin of error for fingerprint evidence. It's either a perfect match or no match at all.

Are print examiners ever wrong? All humans can make mistakes, no matter how good they are at their jobs. However, it is rare that good fingerprint evidence results in a mistaken conclusion. Yet, a poor quality print taken from a crime scene will require even greater skill to analyze. In these cases, one print expert may challenge the conclusions of another in a court.

Computer-based print matching systems use mathematical formulas to pinpoint specific areas of comparison. As few as seven ridge characteristics in the same position are needed for a positive identification. Computer analysis allows large numbers of prints to be quickly compared. This type of analysis means that suspects can be linked to any unsolved crime on record for which prints exist.

ON THE CASE:

THE INVISIBLE PRINT THAT HELPED CATCH A KILLER

On October 1, 1993, 12-year-old Polly Klaas and her two best friends were having a slumber party at Polly's home in Petaluma, California. A stranger wearing a bandana and carrying a knife came into Polly's bedroom through an open window, surprising the three girls.

Even though Polly's mother was sleeping in the next bedroom, the stranger managed to tie up Polly and her two friends. Then, carrying Polly, he escaped from

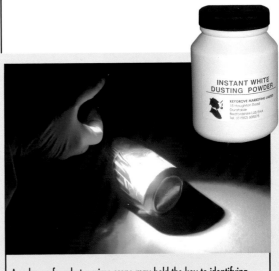

A soda can found at a crime scene may hold the key to identifying a suspect. Dusting the can with fluorescent powder and then looking at the can under a "black" light might show latent prints.

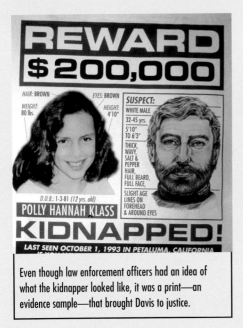

Even though law enforcement officers had an idea of what the kidnapper looked like, it was a print—an evidence sample—that brought Davis to justice.

the house. Polly's friends worked themselves free, then called 911 and described the man the best they could. By the time the police arrived, the girls had told Polly's mother what had happened. Unfortunately, the police couldn't find any useful evidence in the bedroom. Polly was gone, and no one had an idea where she was or who had taken her.

The police called the FBI in San Francisco, and a special forensics team called the Evidence Response Team (ERT) came to the scene. These highly trained evidence recovery experts use the latest technology to try to find evidence that might be missed by using more regular crime scene evidence techniques. In this case, they used a fluorescent powder to "dust" for fingerprints. They dusted any surface that might hold a print. Then, they turned on a light that emitted Ultraviolet or UV rays. The UV light picked up a handprint glowing on the rail of the bunk bed in Polly's bedroom.

A national database of palm prints brought up some possible matches. In the end, a fingerprint expert was able to match the palm print to the palm print of Richard Allen Davis, a man who had gone to prison before for kidnapping. Davis was on parole and law enforcement officers quickly arrested him. Davis confessed to killing Polly and told police where he had buried her body. Without the palm print evidence, Davis probably would have walked free. He was convicted of kidnapping and murder, and he was sentenced to death.

Davis is currently on Death Row in California's San Quentin Prison.

Time-lapse photography shows what happens as a bullet, or slug, enters then exits an object — in this case, a lemon! The bullet is traveling at about 1,100 feet per second!

irearms is the word used by the police and forensics experts to describe guns and ammunition. When found at a crime scene, guns and bullets can provide important evidence—if you know how to "read" them. Crime lab firearms units have the knowledge and technology to make this kind of evidence tell its story.

The mechanics of weapons and bullets

There are two basic types of firearms manufactured today: hand-held types and shoulder types, which include shotguns, rifles, and repeating rifles. Hand-held guns shoot either one bullet at a time or a series of bullets, one after the other. Shotguns shoot a spray of small pellets, rifles usually shoot one large bullet at a time and have to be reloaded after each shot, and repeating rifles shoot a series of bullets, one after the other.

A gunshot happens in a fraction of a second and with incredible speed. A bullet can pass right through or even lodge in any number of solid objects. In the case of a homicide, that object is a human body.

When bullets and cartridge casings are found at a crime scene, they become evidence.

The challenge for detectives is to prove that the slug (bullet) found at a crime scene came from a particular weapon that was fired by a particular person. That's where the firearms crime lab experts come in. They speak the language of guns and bullets. A bullet or cartridge case can carry a wealth of information—even if the gun that fired them is nowhere to be found.

This semi-automatic weapon can fire one bullet after another. The rounds are stored in a structure called a magazine that fits into the gun's handle.

MUZZLE OF THE GUN BARREL

A gun's "fingerprint"

During the eighteenth century, weapons makers discovered that putting raised spiral ridges in gun and rifle barrels made the bullets spin. This improved the accuracy of the weapon and made it easier for a shooter to hit a target.

More than two hundred years later, crime lab specialists are making good use of this change when analyzing firearms evidence.

The lead, or mixture of lead and another metal, used to make a bullet is softer than the material used to make a gun's barrel. Because of this, the raised spiral ridges, or grooves, in the barrel mark the bullet's surface as the bullet spins along it. Each weapon makes its own unique pattern of grooves on a bullet fired from that weapon. Each weapon also marks the cartridge in unique ways. These markings are a type of "fingerprint" that allow the crime lab technician to match a gun to a bullet or a cartridge case.

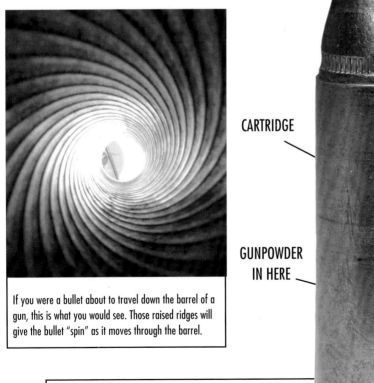

BULLET

CARTRIDGE

GUNPOWDER IN HERE

CAP

If you were a bullet about to travel down the barrel of a gun, this is what you would see. Those raised ridges will give the bullet "spin" as it moves through the barrel.

Lead bullets are mostly used for sport or target-shooting pistols and rifles. The bullets for military rifles and automatic weapons have a lead or steel core but are enclosed in an aluminum or other metal mixture jacket. They travel down the barrel much more quickly.

MECHANICS OF A GUN SHOT

- A bullet is inserted in a metal case called a cartridge. Behind the bullet is a small compartment that holds gunpowder. The cartridge sits in the barrel of the gun.

- The base of the cartridge holds a small cup called a primer. When struck sharply, this primer produces a small spark.

- When a gun's trigger is pulled, a part of the weapon called the firing pin strikes the primer, which sparks and starts burning the gunpowder (in the cartridge).

- As the gunpowder burns, it builds up pressure. Finally, the pressure is great enough that the bullet "shoots" out of the barrel of the gun.

Modern firearms are usually made in factories in large quantities and to certain specifications. The goal is that every gun of a particular model looks and operates the same; each gun has the same barrel, and the inside of each gun's barrel, or its bore, should be the same. Each gun of a particular design should also use the same size, or caliber, bullets. The caliber of a bullet is based on the bore's diameter. A bullet shot from a particular design of gun will always have a particular pattern of marks on the bullet and cartridge casing. Also, each gun will leave its own individual marks on a bullet and cartridge. In the crime lab, the patterns of marks are the first things the specialists examine.

A firearms expert compares two bullets using a comparison microscope. Each bullet is in its own holder, which can be turned in any number of directions. Sometimes, a bullet is misshapen or flattened from entering into a body. An experienced firearms examiner may still be able to find identifying marks on the bullet. The markings (seen on screen) will be kept on file in the "Bulletproof" database.

Firearms tools

A firearms crime lab relies on two important tools. The first is a comparison microscope. This is a powerful microscope that allows two bullets or cartridge cases to be viewed side-by-side. If a bullet has been recovered from a crime scene, a firearms expert can compare markings on the evidence bullet to a bullet test-fired from a suspect's gun. If the markings on the two bullets match up, the expert knows the suspect's gun was used to fire the evidence bullet.

Computers are also used to analyze firearm evidence. Databases holding images of thousands of different types of bullets, cartridge casings, barrel types, and other weapon components can be used to compare to evidence samples found at crime scenes. Images of evidence bullets and cartridge casings can also be stored. If the weapon that fired them is recovered at a later date, a match can be made!

The largest database is called Integrated Ballistics Identification System (IBIS). It is

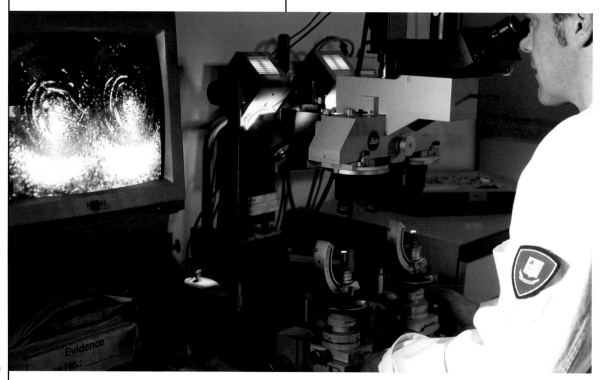

sponsored by the Bureau of Alcohol, Tobacco and Firearms (ATF). IBIS is comprised of two important databases. One is called "Bulletproof" and is used to store bullet images. The other is called "Brasscatcher"—it is used to store images of cartridge cases.

Test-firing weapons

When a weapon recovered from a crime scene comes into the firearms lab for analysis, the request is usually to see if bullets found at the crime scene were shot from that weapon. To test this, it is necessary to shoot a bullet from the weapon and compare it to a bullet found at the crime scene.

When test firing the gun, the firearms specialists need to make sure that the test bullet is not marked by hitting a hard surface at the lab. If the bullet material is very soft, the weapon will be fired into a tank of water. The firing action will mark the bullet with the marks needed to make a comparison, but the water will not deform the bullet further. If the bullet material is harder, it might be fired into thick cotton pads or even containers of sand. In both cases, the test bullet is then compared to the bullet found at the crime scene.

Residue tells a story

A suspect swears she was being attacked and that she shot her victim at close range as an act of self-defense. The suspect's life was in danger, and she felt there was nothing else she could do. The crime scene evidence isn't clear, so the detectives turn to the firearms lab for help. The officers send along evidence bags containing the suspect's gun and the victim's shirt which shows the

This bullet shows the individual markings made by the gun that fired it.

Firearms experts may discharge (shoot) a handgun into a water tank. The bullets enter the water but keep their shape, unlike if they had been fired into a hard material, such as wood. The bullets in the water tank can then be retrieved and their markings compared with bullets found at the crime scene.

hole where the bullet passed through and entered the victim's body.

The firearms examiner will first shoot the weapon at a series of thick cardboard targets that have pieces of fabric attached that are similar to the shirt. When weapons are fired, small pieces of unburned gunpowder blow out of the gun's barrel. The pieces of gunpowder land on the target in a particular pattern according to the distance between the gun and the test material. Each time the examiner shoots, it will be from a different distance. After a shot, the examiner will observe the density and the diameter of gunpowder residue surrounding the hole.

The firearms examiner will be able to figure out almost the exact distance from which the suspect's gun was fired by comparing the amounts of gunpowder residue on the different targets to the amount found on the victim's shirt.

The measurements and residue evidence from the lab will help the detectives determine if the suspect fired the gun from close range or from a distance.

Finding missing numbers

Every firearm has a unique serial number stamped into it. Criminals sometimes try to remove this number by scraping it off. What they don't realize is that the process of stamping the firearm's serial number actually creates a deeper impression than can be seen with the naked eye. So, when a weapon arrives at the crime lab with a serial number that has been filed off, the firearms examiner knows exactly what to do.

First, the examiner polishes the metal on the serial number plate down even farther until it is a smooth strip of metal. Then, the examiner applies a solution of copper salts and hydrochloric acid. This solution acts on the metal to bring up the serial number long enough that the examiner can photograph it.

As the solution dries, the number disappears once more. But that's not a problem—the crime lab has the information they need!

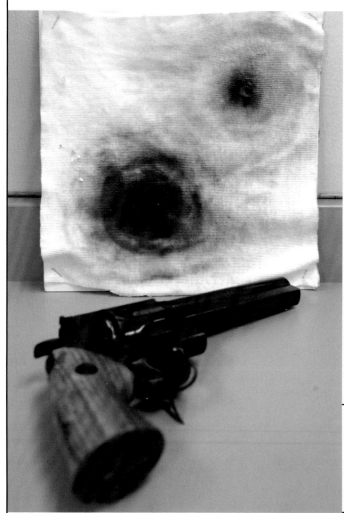

This handgun has been fired at a piece of cloth. The distance between the muzzle and the cloth has been changed with each test shot. The firearms expert can see what the pattern from the discharge looks like at different distances from the target. This can be used as evidence during a trial.

ON THE CASE:

FIREARMS CASE STUDY

As of December, 2005, the Houston Texas Police Department had reached over five hundred "hits." By April 2006, the Detroit, Michigan Police Department had reached 100 "hits" of their own. The "hits" refer to the number of times the police departments have been able to match ballistic evidence such as weapons, cartridge casings, and bullets to images stored in a powerful ATF firearms evidence network called the Integrated Ballistic Identification System (IBIS).

IBIS is part of the Alcohol, Tobacco and Firearms' (ATF's) National Integrated Ballistics Information Network (NIBIN). Here's how it works. Every time a weapon or other piece of firearms evidence is recovered from a crime scene, the crime lab enters the evidence data into NIBIN. If the evidence is a weapon, the crime lab will do test firings of that weapon. They will retrieve the bullets and cartridge casings, then scan images of them into IBIS and then NIBIN. Once the information is entered into the system, any other law enforcement agency that is also on NIBIN can compare their crime scene ballistic evidence with what is in the database. This technology allows law enforcement officers to do in hours what might have taken weeks, months, or longer. They can find out if a weapon picked up at a crime scene has been used in any other crimes anywhere in the U.S. Knowing this gives law enforcement a possible lead to help solve a crime. In Boston, Massachusetts, the police department was able to link one handgun to fifteen shooting incidents that took place in four different areas across two states!

The ATF and other agencies would like to see all weapons automatically entered into IBIS at the time they are manufactured. This would mean collecting data on millions of weapons already owned, and on the new weapons manufactured each year. If they could do it, though, it would be a huge help when it came time to try to track a weapon, bullet, or other ballistic evidence to a crime and, hopefully, a criminal.

A shoulder-type hunting rifle with cartridges of pellets. The gun's serial number is just visible at the bottom of the picture.

In the early 1900s, an interesting idea was proposed by Dr. Edmond Locard, the director of the world's first crime lab in Lyon, France. Dr. Locard believed that there is no such thing as a clean contact between objects. He said that if two bodies or objects come into contact, there will always be some transfer of material. That material is what criminalists now call trace evidence.

Dr. Edmond Locard's hypothesis that all contact between objects will result in some type of trace evidence has been one of the most useful concepts in crime lab science.

Forensic scientists over the years have operated on the idea that Locard's idea is true. Something, somewhere in the crime scene will link the crime to the person who committed the crime. The item that provides the link may be very small: a paint chip, a clothing fiber, a hair, a piece of rope—all of these things are considered trace evidence. They are also all things that can be, and are, analyzed in a crime lab.

Toxicology

The word "toxic" means deadly or involving something poisonous. Toxicology is the study of poisons and it can cover a wide range of substances. Some poisons, such as weed-killers, pesticides, and household cleansers, are found in almost any hardware store or grocery store. Other poisons are found in nature, such as certain mushrooms or plants. Drugs and alcohol are also poisons, when taken in large amounts.

When a homicide case involves toxic substances, samples such as skin, hair,

The beautiful foxglove plant is also very toxic. The same holds true for certain types of fungus, like mushrooms. Some mushrooms are so toxic that eating even small amounts can kill an adult human being.

or blood will arrive at the crime lab. Sometimes, the crime lab might have an idea of what they're looking for in the sample. For instance, a crime scene may have a victim that shows symptoms of suffocation. If the victim was found in a closed garage with the automobile engine running, it might indicate that the person died of carbon monoxide poisoning. This information will be in the crime scene report. The crime lab's first task will be to test for high levels of carboxyhemoglobin (COHb). This substance is present when carbon monoxide gas molecules bind to hemoglobin molecules. Hemoglobin is found in red blood cells. If the test results show that the concentration of COHb in the blood sample is more than 50%, it is likely that the victim died of carbon monoxide poisoning.

High-technology analysis

Most of the substances found at a crime scene are complex chemical mixtures. The crime lab must be able to break down the mixtures and identify every separate chemical or substance in a sample.

In the toxicology lab, chromatographs and mass spectrometers are used to carry out these tasks. Both instruments use line graphs to show the data. Gas chromatographs are the most common type used, and they are often paired with a mass spectrometer. This testing system is called GC/MS.

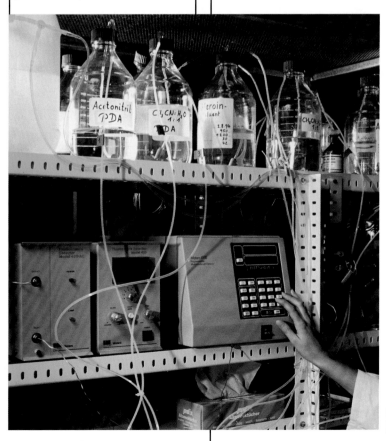

Liquid chromatography can be used in crime labs to help identify specific drugs. The drug sample is injected into the sample line (the plastic tubing). Under high pressure, the chemicals carry the drug molecules into columns packed with beads. There, the chemicals in the unknown drugs will separate out, making it possible to identify them.

Pills and capsules found at crime scenes are important evidence. Drugs, such as heroine or cocaine, might be identified at the scene with chemicals found in an investigator's kit. Other drugs, though, will arrive in the crime lab for analysis.

CG/MS testing

The toxicology specialist will first prepare the sample of blood, urine, or tissue by dissolving it in a very acidic or basic solution. Then, the dissolved material is injected into a hollow tube. A gas, such as hydrogen or helium, is flowing through the tube as well. These gases are called "carrier gases." They mix in, or "carry," the sample in the tube. They also help to separate the sample. Helium is the gas most often used in gas chromatography because it can be safely heated and works with many types of detectors. The tube coils into a small chamber that heats the sample in the tube. As the sample travels farther along the tube, some of the chemicals in the sample will be traveling faster than others. As the gas and sample continue along the tube, they pass a detector that identifies what specific chemicals are present in the sample. The next step involves the spectrometer.

The mass spectrometer is linked to the gas chromatograph. The sample passes from the chromatograph to the spectrometer, where it is blasted with electrons. This causes the chemicals to break into charged particles. Like the chromatograph, the spectrometer has a detector that counts the number of charged particles that have a specific mass. This is how the spectrometer identifies exactly how much of each chemical is in the sample.

The analysis from the GC/MS is displayed as a line graph. The toxicology expert will compare the sample line graph to graphs of known chemical substances. In this way, the specific types and amounts of chemicals in the evidence sample are identified. The GC/MS analysis might show the presence of several different chemicals which, when combined, could be weed killer. Alternatively, they might identify a pure poison, such as arsenic, or strychnine.

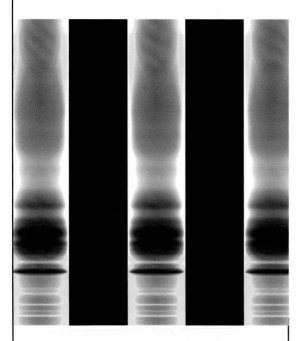

The separation of different chemicals in this chromatography sample is shown by bands of colors. The sample has been mixed with another liquid and moved across a material such as paper. Different chemicals move across the paper at different rates and will separate in unique ways.

HIDING MURDER

In the past, poison was a favorite method of murder because poisoning often causes the same symptoms as other conditions or diseases.

- Putting a little piece of a plant, like poison hemlock, into someone's drink would cause a death that looked like suffocation.

- Strychnine was another favorite! Made from a shrub found in India, just 1/50 of a gram of this substance was enough to cause a death that looked like the result of the disease tetanus.

Murder by poison was once very effective. Today, sophisticated lab equipment has made it possible to identify even the smallest trace of poison in the body of a murder victim.

ON THE CASE:

THE TYLENOL MURDERS

In 1982, seven people in the Chicago, Illinois area died under mysterious circumstances. Eventually, it was found that they had all taken a pain relief medicine, called Tylenol, that was mixed with cyanide, a very powerful poison. The killer had unscrewed bottles of Tylenol, then opened the capsules, added small pellets of cyanide, and put the capsules back together. The cyanide meant sudden death for the seven victims.

The victims included a twelve-year-old girl, a twenty-seven-year-old man, and a mother of a newborn baby. Three of the victims were from the same family. At the hospital where the three family members were taken, Dr. Thomas Kim was very suspicious that all three seemed to have died from the same cause. He took blood samples and sent them to a lab for testing of a number of different poisons.

Firefighters in another area of Chicago were talking about the four deaths that had happened in their areas—all sudden deaths with no apparent cause. The firefighters knew that the twelve-year-old girl had taken Tylenol for her cold and wondered if any other victims had taken the same medicine. One of the firefighters telephoned the paramedics who had responded to the deaths of the three family members and asked if the three victims had also taken Tylenol. To everyone's surprise, the connection was made—all the victims had taken Tylenol capsules. The police sent samples of the capsules they had taken from the victims' homes to a toxicology lab.

The lab quickly identified the presence of cyanide.

The killer was never found, but the poisonings suddenly stopped. One result of the Tylenol poisoning tragedy is that it led to the "tamper proof" caps and covers used today for over-the-counter medicines.

Crime lab technicians test blood for drugs, alcohol, toxins (poisons), and chemicals.

Did this car roll over because it was hit by another vehicle? Did it hit some object and flip? Paint samples taken from the vehicle, the concrete, and any place else that came into contact with the car will be analyzed to find answers to these questions.

A crime lab technician may look to see how the jagged edges of paint samples will fit together. How the paint broke apart can help an evidence expert determine facts such as how fast the vehicle was going when it hit another object or person.

Painting a picture

Paint chips can be important pieces of the puzzle when solving a crime that involves vehicles and people. It might seem almost impossible to get much information from a tiny sliver of paint on a hit-and-run victim's clothing or from a car involved in a wreck, but with modern crime lab equipment, the impossible becomes possible. That one paint chip could lead detectives to a vehicle involved in the crime!

One way to match a paint chip to a vehicle is called the physical match method. If police officers have a part of a suspect car with a missing chip of paint, the paint chip sample can be fitted into the missing area. The crime lab examiner would need to photograph the paint chip sample and the car part, then write up a detailed description of every step of the matching method so that it could be understood by a non-lab person—such as an attorney or a jury member.

More often than not, however, the evidence sample is likely to be paint chips taken from the scene of a crime where the vehicle is not available. In the case of a hit-and-run accident, the paint sample might be somewhere on the victim's body. When this type of sample arrives in the crime lab, it is normally examined using a powerful microscope. The microscope will show what the crime lab experts already know: Paint chips have several layers.

Layers of information

The first layer is the first coat that went on the car, usually a gray paint called primer. Then, another layer might be the first coat of colored paint applied to the vehicle. Yet another layer would be the top coat of paint or a gloss coating put on over the paint. The structure of the layers, the thickness of each layer, and other physical characteristics are visible under the microscope.

The images of the paint chip layers can be compared with identifying images provided by car manufacturers. These images are stored in computer databases. As with fingerprint and firearms comparisons, paint chips can be compared on-screen with known samples.

The chemical story

A gas chromatograph and spectrometer might also be used to analyze a paint chip. In this case, the paint sample is dissolved in a liquid and run through the chromatograph. The paint sample is broken down into all the chemicals that went into making the paint. This will include materials such as pigments, which are used to hold in the paint's color. Each type of paint uses a particular amount and type of pigment. Breaking down the paint sample in this way creates a "fingerprint" for each layer of the paint, making comparison with a known paint type even more accurate.

Knowing the paint type means that detectives can also find out who made the paint and the make of car on which the paint was used.

Eventually, a little scrap of paint might lead detectives to the specific car used in the crime.

A small piece of paint from another vehicle was left behind when it collided with this car. Even though the paint chip held in the tweezers is small, it may have a number of different layers. Maybe the car had been painted a number of times. This information is useful to detectives trying to track down a particular vehicle.

Fiber evidence

One of the ways that a suspect can be placed at the scene of a crime is through fiber evidence. A fiber is the smallest unit of cloth or textile material. Fibers can be transferred through contact between a victim and a perpetrator. They can also be transferred between a person and an object or even between two objects. For example, carpet fibers might be transferred onto the sole of a shoe.

Fibers used in clothing, automobile interiors, and furniture fabrics may be man-made, natural, or a combination of the two. Natural fabrics are those made from natural fibers such as silk, wool, cotton, flax, and animal hair. Man-made fabrics are made from fibers such as polyester and nylon. Natural and man-made fibers have their own characteristics that are visible under a microscope.

Fiber evidence coming into the crime lab may come in as individual fibers, pieces of cloth, or entire articles of clothing, such as a shirt. With large samples, the material is attached to a flat surface and the eyepieces of a microscope are directed to the material. This type of microscope looks something like a very large pair of binoculars. By increasing the magnification, the fabric examiner can see the different fibers, their particular diameters, and other identifying characteristics. Cameras linked into the microscope take photographs of what the examiner actually sees. These photos can be printed out or stored in an on-line database for later viewing.

Often, crime lab examiners have only a few small fibers to work with. Along with a high-magnification microscope, examiners may use a method

Crime lab technicians use microscopes and tweezers to collect evidence from bloodstained clothes. The evidence could be hair, fibers from clothing, human skin tissue, or an unknown material. Analyzing this evidence further might link the evidence to suspects, placing them at the crime scene.

called microspectrophotometry. This very long word describes the process of shining a beam of light on the sample while it's under the microscope. The light used might be either visible or infrared light. The examiner sees how the fiber absorbs different parts of the light. The way the fiber absorbs the light varies from one type of fiber to another.

As with some other types of evidence, a fiber sample might be run through a chromatograph to get a reading of the types of chemicals used to make the dye. The chemicals can then be compared to the chemicals listed by different fabric manufacturers. This information may help lead investigators to where the fiber was made. Knowing where and when it was made might provide a link to how it ended up at the crime scene.

Even though it looks like loops of purple and green yarn, this is actually the view magnified through a scanning electron microscope (SEM) of a fabric made from knitted nylon and polyester.

ON THE CASE:

FIBER LEADS TO A KILLER

Between 1979 and 1981, a killer terrorized Atlanta, Georgia. Young men were found strangled, and the only real clue that the police had was the presence of an unusual fiber found on some of the victims' clothing.

Eventually, detectives narrowed their list of suspects down to Wayne Williams, a music promoter living in the Atlanta area. When crime scene investigation teams searched Williams's house and car, they found samples of the same unusual fiber that had been found on some of the victims.

Tests in a crime lab identified the specific structure of the fiber and the materials used to make the fiber.

The fiber was compared to all the fibers made by mills for which the police had reference samples. This comparison enabled detectives to trace the fiber to a carpet manufacturer in Dalton, Georgia. The manufacturer informed police that the particular carpet from which the fibers were taken had only been made in small quantities. This narrowed down the number of possible places where the police would find carpet made with this material.

The police used this information and other fiber evidence, such as clothing fibers, to help convict Wayne Williams for two murders.

Evidence by a hair

Hairs found at a crime scene often provide the link between a crime and a perpetrator. The hair might be from the criminal, the victim, or even pet hair from either individual. Hair easily attaches itself to any number of surfaces—especially clothing and carpet. A single hair may not seem very important, but as evidence, it can be the key to solving a case.

Hairs are mainly made up of a protein called keratin. Keratin is the one thing all hair has in common. After that, there may be dramatic differences. Each species of animal has hair with particular characteristics. These characteristics include specific lengths, shapes, even the internal structure of the hair. Hair is also a main source of DNA evidence, which we will look at in the next chapter.

Like all evidence coming into a crime lab, hair evidence will be documented, and the examiner will review the crime scene report. In most cases, the hair would then be removed from the evidence bag using sterile tweezers and immediately placed under a microscope that might magnify the sample to 1,000 times its original size. Under this level of magnification, a hair looks like a giant tube. To a crime lab technician, the giant tube will have certain traits that will help identify it.

Crime lab scientists can tell the difference between human head hair and human body hair. They can also tell the difference between types of animal hair. Deer hair looks very different from cat hair. Even different breeds of dogs have particular characteristics to their hair. This information would be important if traces of hair from a specific

This Scanning Electron Microscope (SEM) image shows hair shafts growing from the surface of human skin. SEM images are black and white, but can be artificially colored (as here) to help highlight details.

Seen this close, it's clear that dog hair looks very different from human hair. The outer layer of each hair is made up of overlapping scales. The scales may prevent a dog's hair from becoming tightly tangled or matted.

Investigators at a crime scene may find this hair snagged on some sharp wire. Is it human hair or animal hair? It may be evidence, but they won't know until the hair sample is sent to the crime lab and analyzed.

breed of dog were found on both a crime suspect and the victim.

Loser by a hair

In the case of the kidnapping and murder of Australian schoolboy Graeme Thorne, investigators found animal hairs on the boy's clothing. Examination of the hairs revealed that they were from a Pekingese dog. When the police examined the car of a suspect, Stephen Bradley, they found the same type of dog hairs. A local veterinary hospital was able to confirm that Stephen Bradley owned a Pekingese. The tiniest amount of trace evidence was responsible for putting Bradley behind bars for kidnapping and murder.

DNA technology has become the hot topic in forensic science. This is because DNA analysis is one of the most powerful tools available to criminalists in helping prove the guilt or innocence of a suspect. It can tie a person to the scene of a crime beyond the shadow of a doubt. Equally important, it can be used to prevent an innocent person from paying for a crime they didn't commit.

In 1984, a mentally challenged man named Earl Washington confessed to the rape and murder of a Virginia woman. Although Washington later said he wasn't guilty, he was tried, convicted, and sentenced to death. At the time of the crime, some of the perpetrator's body fluids were collected from the victim. However, the technology was not available to analyze those fluids and prove Washington's innocence or guilt. By the time DNA evidence helped free him, Earl Washington had spent sixteen years in prison. Fourteen of those years were on death row.

In 1953, scientists James Watson and Francis Crick created a model of a DNA molecule. Called the "double-helix," the model showed that each strand of the DNA molecule was a pattern for the other. Most important were the discoveries that DNA molecules can reproduce themselves without changing and that they are present in every cell of a living organism.

Imagine that you've been convicted of a crime that you didn't commit! Modern DNA analysis is helping free innocent people while also finding the real offenders and bringing them to justice.

A boost from technology

DNA stands for deoxyribonucleic acid. This is a strand of coded information inside every single one of our cells. Except for identical twins, no two people have the same DNA. This fact is of great importance to law enforcement.

Even though fingerprints are also unique, even for twins, fingerprints only come from fingers. DNA, on the other hand, can be found in everything from fingernail clippings to the sweat in a hatband! For example, a kidnapper licks the envelope containing a ransom note. The kidnapper's DNA can be lifted from the saliva left on that envelope. A homicide victim is tied with rope. Skin cells scraped from that rope might belong to the murderer. Even a single strand of hair caught in a pair of eyeglasses can be used to collect DNA and identify an individual.

Whatever the crime scene investigators find and bag, the DNA analysis experts are ready for the evidence when the sample arrives in the lab.

Analyzing DNA in the crime lab

The first step is separating DNA evidence samples from other types of crime scene evidence samples. In order for DNA test results to be correct, it is very important that the DNA samples are handled properly while in the crime lab. For example, DNA samples are carefully refrigerated to reduce the likelihood that the samples will begin to break down.

Crime lab technicians will make sure that the samples are correctly labeled and have the right dates on the containers. As with any piece of evidence, all handling of the samples in any way is documented from the moment the samples arrive.

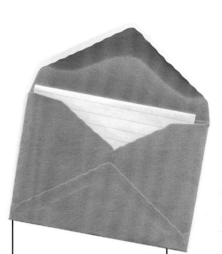

Crime Scene Investigators can collect possible DNA evidence from many sources: The licked flap of an envelope, the neck of a bottle, and sweat on our clothes.

Crime labs analyzing DNA samples use DNA Extraction Kits to extract the DNA from the biological evidence sample, such as a sample of blood or saliva. The extracted material is then run through a testing and analysis process.

There are several different types of tests that can be run to analyze DNA. One test is called gel electrophoresis. In this method, the DNA strand is cut into smaller pieces by an enzyme that acts like chemical "scissors." These smaller pieces are then placed into a special gel. High voltage electric current is applied to the gel. This causes the different pieces of DNA to move through the gel. The shorter pieces move more quickly through the gel than longer pieces. The result is that the pieces sort themselves by length. Each piece represents its own code of information.

The pieces are then transferred to a very thin sheet of nylon. A radioactive marker links up with DNA pieces that have particular codes. The nylon sheet is then placed on a special film that reacts to X-rays. When the film is developed, the DNA fragments appear. They look like a series of small bars with spaces in between, much like

DNA experts may use a magnifying glass to study the details of a DNA sample. The scientist is looking for a particular sequence of chemicals that form the code for a specific section of the DNA strand. The readout in the scientist's hand is the result of a DNA test done using gel electrophoresis.

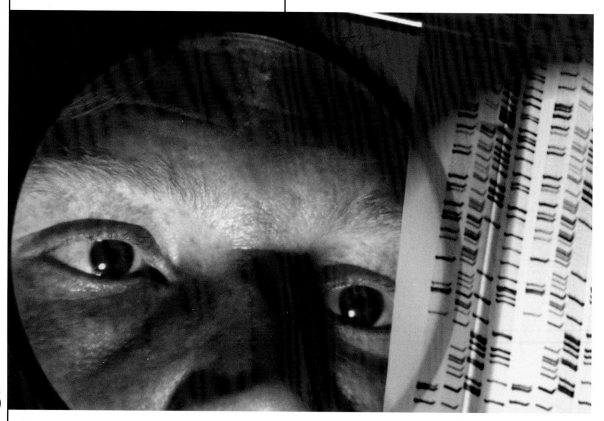

the barcode you might find on a product in the store. In the same way a barcode identifies a particular product, the DNA sequence identifies a particular individual.

Another, faster, method involves taking the DNA sample and causing the DNA to copy itself many times. This makes for a larger sample. Then, the sample goes through the gel electrophoresis process. This time, though, an instrument looks for the number of times a particular group of DNA appears. This produces a computer-generated code that is expressed in numbers. Because it is in numbers, it is easier for the information to be stored in computer databases.

Whichever test is chosen, the DNA analyst will be very careful that the correct test procedures are followed. This ensures that the results will be accurate and useful as evidence.

Creating a DNA profile

The information taken from DNA analysis is used to create a DNA Profile. The profile is a record of the unique information that pertains to any particular person. DNA Profiles are stored in national and international databases. One of these databases is called the Combined DNA Index System (CODIS). DNA profiles created from crime scene evidence can be compared to the DNA profiles

of convicted offenders. All fifty states in the United States have laws that require DNA samples to be taken from certain types of offenders. Profiles are run on these samples and stored in the CODIS database. Some of the databases have hundreds of thousands of DNA profiles that can be called up in a matter of seconds. The databases are critical because, as with all other types of criminal evidence, there must always be a means to compare information from a suspect against what might already be known. When a suspect's DNA has been used to create a DNA profile, it can be matched against DNA profiles already in the database.

Crime lab experts will be able to extract DNA for testing from this blood-soaked glove, which was found at a crime scene.

DNA samples are often taken at the time of a suspect's arrest. These samples may be obtained from a cotton swab wiped on the inside of a suspect's cheek.

ON THE CASE:

DNA CAPTURES KILLER AFTER 10 YEARS

During 1990, a killer in Goldsboro, North Carolina, was targeting the elderly. In March of that year, an elderly woman was raped and almost murdered. She was saved because her daughter happened to come home early. The next victim wasn't so lucky.

Hattie Bonner was seventy-four years old when she was raped and suffocated. In October of that year, the killer struck again. This time, he broke into the home of Al and Thelma Bowen. Seventy-six-year-old Thelma was raped and stabbed to death. Al, her seventy-eight-year-old husband, was also stabbed. In an attempt to cover up the crime, the killer set fire to the Bowens' house.

In the case of each murder, body fluids were collected from the victims. Some of the fluids included those of the perpetrator. A DNA analysis was run. The results from the analysis showed that the same man had committed all three rapes and the murders. However,

even though law enforcement officials had DNA proof that it was one criminal doing all the horrible crimes, they didn't know who that criminal might be.

A serologist is a scientist who examines physical evidence for the presence or absence of biological fluids, such as blood. Here, a serologist prepares a sample for a DNA test. The serologist's latex gloves, face mask, goggles, and hair net help prevent contamination of the sample.

For ten years, the Goldsboro Police Department and the crime laboratory kept hoping for a match. They never forgot the crimes and the suffering of the elderly victims.

Over the next few years, DNA technology became more accurate. There was less possibility of error through contamination of the sample or of the sample breaking down during testing. The crime lab retested the fluids taken from the victims. This time, they entered the DNA profiles into the North Carolina DNA database.

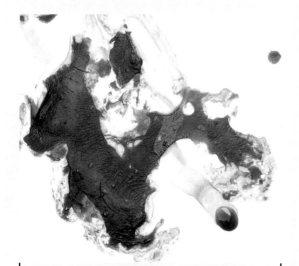

An evidence sample may have the blood of the victim and the perpetrator blended in one big stain. However, when the blood is separated from the sample, the DNA tests that follow will identify that there are two blood samples present instead of one.

In 2001, they found a match. Lynwood Forte had been convicted in 1996 of firing a shot into a home where people were living. Being convicted of this type of crime meant that the perpetrator had to have a DNA profile taken and entered into the North Carolina database. When law enforcement officers saw that there was a DNA profile match, they arrested Forte. He was brought in for questioning and had to give a blood sample. The sample was analyzed and found to match the crime scene evidence from ten years earlier.

When Forte was told about the DNA evidence, he confessed to all the crimes. He was then convicted of the rapes and murders and executed.

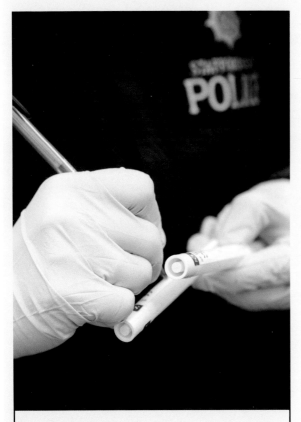

A police officer labels DNA samples taken from a suspect. Buccal cells are often used in DNA analysis. These cells can be obtained from the inside of a person's cheek. A buccal swab kit includes plastic swab sticks that are gently scraped against the inside of the cheek.

TECHNOLOGY & SCIENCE

Ten years may seem like a long time to solve a crime. The truth is that there are some crimes that have remained unsolved a lot longer than that. One of the reasons that "cold," or seemingly unsolvable, cases finally get solved is that the technology has been developed that can answer certain questions.

Sometimes these answers depend on instruments being more accurate or needing less of a sample to test. Sometimes, the technology may be there, but advances in science haven't caught up. For example, we now have more powerful microscopes than ever before. Scientific studies may uncover more and more things to see with such microscopes.

When it comes to crime lab science and technology:

- *The need to understand more about science pushes the development of technology to achieve that understanding.*
- *The more scientists understand, the greater technology will have to be to allow scientists to explore further.*
- *Science and technology are joined together. As one gets better, so does the other.*

A science laboratory will always be a place where exciting equipment can be found. A crime science laboratory is even more exciting because the equipment and scientific methods are being used to help solve crimes. As technology advances, the options available to criminalists will become ever more sophisticated, and ever more accurate.

One tiny drop of blood. One fingerprint. Either of these things can be used to identify a person beyond a reasonable doubt. In the future, though, forensic scientists may look back and see these methods of identification as very old-fashioned!

The future crime lab

Chromatographs have been used for many years to run different tests within the crime lab. The newest versions of this instrument are now so sensitive that they can produce a very complete chemical breakdown of a drop of sweat. These instruments are also so accurate that the readout of an analysis will be as detailed as that for a fingerprint. Some crime lab scientists believe that it won't be too long before there are instruments that will be able to analyze a person's body odor and identify all the tiny trace amounts of chemicals present in that odor.

Imagine speaking into a digital voice recorder and seeing your voice transformed into a one-of-a-kind graph. How about a scanner that takes instantaneous measurements of the retina in your eye? These may seem like technologies that exist far in the future, but they really exist right now. Scientific instruments and advanced computer programming are changing the face of the crime lab. As crime lab science becomes more

advanced, crime lab scientists will need to be extra careful to follow good scientific procedure. As testing methods become more sophisticated, it will become even more important that evidence samples are handled in the right way to avoid any kind of contamination and even more important that samples are stored in the correct way and kept at particular temperatures for the tests to be right. Skilled crime lab specialists will be needed to take advantage of the technology available.

And, as more and more law enforcement agencies come to rely on crime lab testing results, the crime lab specialist will have greater responsibility. A crime lab scientist's specialty may be DNA analysis. It might be fingerprint identification or gas chromatography. Whatever the specialty may be, others will be counting on that person to practice good scientific methods: observation, hypothesis, experimentation, data collection, and drawing a conclusion.

BIOMETRIC SCAN PROGRESS:

CARD: VALID

IRIS: COMPLETE

RETINA: 62%

PATTERN MATCHING:

IN PROGRESS

AUTHENTICATION: PENDING

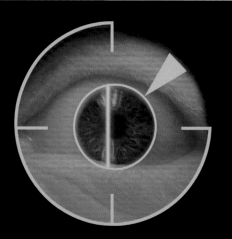

The retina is a thin layer of cells that line the back wall of the eyeball. Each person's retina has hundreds of blood vessels that form a unique pattern. The human retina stays the same from birth to death.

Scientists working in the crime labs of the future will have even greater advances in technology to help them analyze evidence. This means that crime lab specialists will continue to play an important role in helping the police identify those who commit crimes.

SAY IT AGAIN, PLEASE

Scientists are discovering that voices, like fingerprints, have characteristics that can be used to identify people.

• A voiceprint is made by recording a few seconds of a person's voice on a tape recorder. The recording is then analyzed to identify all the different frequencies present in the particular voice. A voiceprint can be displayed on a computer screen and viewed in the same way as a fingerprint.

• The voiceprints of people convicted of telephone crimes, such as terrorist threats, could be stored and checked in the future for matches in the same way as fingerprint and DNA databases are used.

LOOKING TO THE FUTURE

The idea for retina scans has been around since the 1930s, but only recently has the technology become available to allow the scans to be done quickly and accurately.

• Retina scans can be useful in airports and other high security areas. The scans would make it impossible for a person to try to slip through while using another person's identity.

ON THE CASE:

WHERE HAVE YOU BEEN?

Think you're ready to be a crime lab specialist? See if you can draw conclusions based on trace evidence you find on a friend or relative.

You will need:

- Tweezers
- Hand lens or magnifying glass
- 10 small resealable plastic bags
- Notebook and sticky labels
- Pencil or pen, and a marker pen

Tweezers may not seem "high-tech" but they are the most common instrument used to handle certain types of evidence without also contaminating that evidence.

You will need to check:

- Clothes
- Shoes—remember to check the soles
- Hands

Look for:

- Any kind of hair (does the person have a dog or a cat?)
- Plant leaves or burrs
- Particles of dirt or chalky dust
- Clothing fibers

Each piece of "evidence" must be in its own small bag. Don't contaminate!! Keep everything separate.

Use the tweezers to transfer each piece of trace evidence from the "scene" into its own bag. Avoid using your hands to touch anything at all, even if it's a large piece of evidence, such as a stone in someone's shoe.

Label each bag with the following information:

- Date and time you collected the sample
- Where you collected the sample
- What the sample is
- The name of the person from whom you got the sample

Observe

Using the hand lens, closely examine each sample. Draw out a label (see right). Fill in the sections with details about the evidence you are observing. For example, what color is the hair or fiber? What size is a stone from a shoe?

Make sure to write down the date and times when you began and ended your examination of each piece of evidence.

Analyze

Draw conclusions from the evidence you have collected. For example, if you collected a hair sample, does it belong to the person on whom you found it or to one of their sisters or brothers? Does it belong to their pet?

For a stone sample from a shoe, does the stone match any gravel around your home or school? Where did it come from? The answer will help you decide where you or the other person has been.

In a notebook or on a label attached to your evidence bags, make a separate record for each evidence sample you collect.

EVIDENCE SAMPLE NO: 3

DATE & TIME OBSERVATIONS BEGIN
10/22/06   3:54 p.m.

OBSERVATIONS (color, measurements of sample)
A small stone; oval shaped. Pale brown color (like toffee). It measures 1" x 0.5". A black mark on one end.

PLACE SAMPLE FOUND
In the sole of Sam Brown's sneaker, left foot, center of the heel.

DATE & TIME OBSERVATIONS ENDED
10/22/06   4:00 p.m.

Police Force_____
Identifying Mark_____
Court Exhibit No_____
R.-V.-_____

Description_____
_____
_____
_____
_____

Time/Date Seized/Produced_____

Where Seized/Produced_____
_____
_____

Seized/Produced By_____

Signed_____

Incident/Crime No. _____
Major Incident Exhibit No._____
Laboratory Ref._____

A real evidence bag will have a seal that clearly shows if someone tries to open the bag after it's been closed at the crime scene.

A dried leaf or a single cat hair could become evidence linking a particular person to a particular place.

Glossary

attorney: A lawyer. People hire attorneys to speak for them in court proceedings and to give them advice about the law.

carbon monoxide: A colorless, odorless gas that is toxic in high amounts. Carbon monoxide forms when compounds that have carbon in them are burned. Car exhaust is one source of carbon monoxide gas.

criminalists: People who collect, process, and analyze evidence in a crime case. Criminalists can be detectives or civilians, and they often specialize in crime scenes, fingerprints, blood spatter, DNA, firearms (guns and bullets), impressions (tire tracks and shoeprints), tool marks (made by weapons), or other areas.

Crime Scene Investigator (C.S.I.): The person in charge of processing a crime scene. Duties include sealing off the scene, photographing the scene, and collecting evidence. The job title may also be criminalist (see above), crime scene analyst, or, in the United Kingdom, Scene of Crime Officer (S.O.C.O.).

DNA: A molecule that is present in every life form and contains sequences of chemicals that form the "code of life"—the genetic instructions for making a plant, animal, or other organism. The letters stand for Deoxyribonucleic Acid.

evidence: Proof or disproof. Evidence can be physical (such as blood or a weapon) or testimonial (such as witness statements).

forensic: An adjective that means having to do with evidence in an investigation—a crime, an accident, a natural disaster, and so on.

homicide: A manner of death in which one person kills another. According to the law, murder is the most serious type of homicide. Other types of homicide are manslaughter (a less serious charge) and assisted suicide (helping someone die).

hypothesis: An explanation for what might have happened, made on the basis of limited evidence and used as a starting point for further investigation.

infrared light: Invisible light located just below red in the electromagnetic spectrum. (The term "infrared" means "below red.") Special scanners or visual aids are needed to see infrared light.

perpetrator: The person who commits a crime.

radioactive: A substance such as uranium or plutonium that gives off energy in streams of particles.

trace evidence: Evidence such as hair, fibers, dust, soil particles, paint flakes, or other microscopic material that can link a suspect to a place where a crime was committed.

BOOKS

Mystery stories are a great way to learn how to think like a detective, especially the cases of Sherlock Holmes, written by Sir Arthur Conan Doyle. The books below are nonfiction guides.

Bowers, Vivien. *Crime Scene: How Investigators Use Science to Track Down the Bad Guys*. (Maple Tree Press, 2006). How toolmarks and fibers provide evidence, how to detect fake money and forgery, and the ways in which clues, suspects, and victims are connected.

Platt, Richard. *Forensics*. (Kingfisher/Houghton Mifflin, 2005). How to process a crime scene, measure ballistics (bullets and other projectiles), tell counterfeit money from real money, and more.

Wiese, Jim. *Detective Science: 40 Crime-Solving, Case-Breaking, Crook-Catching Activities for Kids*. (Jossey-Bass, 1996). How to collect trace evidence, lift fingerprints, make tooth impressions, and other hands-on activities.

WEB SITES

Access Excellence: The Mystery Spot
www.accessexcellence.org/AE/mspot/
Fictional mysteries that require your use of science to solve them.

CourtTV News: Forensic Files
www.courttv.com/onair/shows/forensicfiles/glossary/1.html
A database of glossary terms, case files, and forensic investigating techniques, such as the use of a Global Positioning System, casting shoe prints, inspecting fingerprints, DNA, hair and fiber evidence, and so on.

FBI Youth
www.fbi.gov/kids/6th12th/6th12th.htm
The FBI's site for kids includes activities and games from the Federal Bureau of Investigation, the U.S. government office that investigates federal crimes.

Who Dunnit?
www.cyberbee.com/whodunnit/crime.html
Online, fictional cases for you to crack.

> **Publisher's note to educators and parents:**
> Our editors have carefully reviewed these Web sites to ensure that they are suitable for children. Many Web sites change frequently, however, and we cannot guarantee that a site's future contents will continue to meet our high standards of quality and educational value. Be advised that children should be closely supervised whenever they access the Internet.

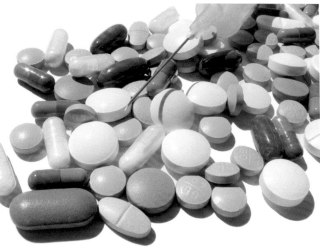

Index